inding North

he sun rises in the e
he sun is just comin
ght hand—you're no
low stretch out your
irection—that's west
orth and your backpac

inding Your Way at Night

t is possible to find north, south, east, and west at night, but first you will have to
ecognize two different star patterns. (Luckily, they look alike.)

One of the most well-known star formations in the Northern Hemisphere is the Big
Dipper. It looks like a large soup ladle or ice cream scoop that is pointing up, away
rom the horizon. The two stars that create the far end of the scoop are known as
Merak and Dubhe. If you draw an imaginary line starting at Merak and continuing

p through Dubhe, you will hit
Polaris, the North Star, which is
he top of the handle of the Little
Dipper. If you walk in the same
direction of that line, you will be
iking north. Keep it on your back
f you need to head south. Let it
est on your right shoulder to hike
vest. And point your left shoulder
oward it to head east.

Jsing Shadows

n the middle of the day, when the sun is directly overhead, it can be challenging
o figure out which direction is east and which direction is west. However, if you
top for a while (this is a perfect moment for a snack) and watch the shadows move
ver a period of time, you can gain a general sense of direction. As time passes, the
hadows will travel from west to east.

Important Compass Features:

1. BASEPLATE It is clear so you can see through it to take bearings (the directions in degrees) from a map underneath.

2. DIRECTION OF TRAVEL ARROW It helps you maintain your path when you are following a bearing.

3. INDEX LINE OR BEARING MARKER Aligned with the direction of travel arrow, it indicates the bearing on the rotating bezel.

4. ORIENTING ARROW It indicates where the magnetic needle should be positioned to follow a bearing.

5. MAGNETIC NEEDLE Usually painted red on its north end, it spins according to the earth's magnetic field and always points to magnetic north.

6. RULER It helps you figure out the actual distance using a map's scale.

7. ROTATING BEZEL Marked from 0 to 360, it converts cardinal directions into degrees.

How to Set Your Bearing

A bearing is a more precise way to describe a direction by using the degrees of a circle. So north is 0, east is 90 degrees, south is 180, and west is 270.

Let's say you are out for a hike and a historic cabin is located a half mile off trail from where you are standing. You need a bearing of 135 degrees (roughly southeast) to reach it.

Keep the compass flat so the compass needle can correctly point to magnetic north. Then follow the steps on the next page.

STEP 1. Find 135 degrees on the rotating bezel and turn it so it aligns with the direction of travel arrow.

STEP 2. Turn your body until the compass needle is inside the orienting arrow. This is often called "putting red Fred in the shed."

STEP 3. Now look at the degree that the travel arrow is pointing to on the compass. If the travel arrow is pointing to 135, you are facing 135 degrees. Walk in the same direction as the direction of travel arrow while keeping red Fred in the shed, and in a half mile you should reach the historic cabin.

Compass Fail!

Before you start walking, make sure it is the red, north-pointing end of the needle that lines up with the orienting arrow. If the other side of the needle is aligned with the orienting arrow, you will end up walking in the opposite direction.

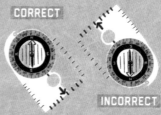

CORRECT

INCORRECT

North Versus North

True north is the geographic north pole, where all longitude lines meet. All maps show true north, usually at the top of the map. A compass needle, however, aligns itself with the earth's magnetic field, so it points to magnetic north, which is not the same as geographic north. The difference between magnetic north and true north is called declination, and it varies depending on where you are located. If you are traveling more than a few hundred yards, you will need to account for declination. Even being off by a single degree can cause you to miss your target by one hundred feet over a mile (forty-nine meters over a kilometer).

Different styles of compasses have different methods for adjusting the declination, so be sure to read through the instructions that come with your navigation tool. The place to find the declination for your given location is the NOAA (National Oceanic and Atmospheric Administration) website. Find the correct declination for your location and reprogram your compass.

What to Pack

SHELTER Important if you get lost and unexpectedly need to spend a night outside, or if you encounter bad weather and need to hunker down.

NAVIGATION TOOL A compass and map or handheld GPS device can help you if you get lost.

LIGHT SOURCE A headlamp or flashlight.

FIRE STARTER Matches or a lighter.

REPAIR OR TOOL KIT A repair kit might include duct tape, a knife, or anything that can fix your gear out in the field.

SUN PROTECTION Sun protection is important on sunny and cloudy days. This could be sunscreen, sunglasses, a hat, lip balm, or clothing that will cover your skin.

EXTRA CLOTHES For those cold, wet, and windy days, the proper amount of insulation might include a jacket, gloves, and a hat. Higher elevations have colder weather, and it often sneaks up on you!

WATER Always take more water than you think you will need.

FOOD Always take more food than you think you will need.

WHISTLE To signal for help in times of distress.

CELL PHONE OR WATCH A smartphone can be a handy multi-tool on the trail that includes a clock, compass, and camera. If you don't pack a cell phone, consider bringing a watch so you can keep track of time.

DUCT TAPE To fix gear, prevent blisters, or use in any other way you might think of. (Duct tape can also be used like moleskin to prevent blisters.)

What to Pack: First Aid

BANDAGES IN A VARIETY OF SIZES: Cover minor cuts and protect against infection.

GAUZE PADS AND ADHESIVE: Cover burns and larger scrapes and apply pressure to stop bleeding.

ALCOHOL PADS: Disinfect wounds.

ANTIBIOTIC OINTMENT: Prevent infection in minor scrapes or cuts.

LIGHTWEIGHT SYRINGE: Flush wounds with clean water.

ASPIRIN OR IBUPROFEN: Treat pain, fever, and inflammation.

ANTIHISTAMINE (SUCH AS BENADRYL): Treat allergic reactions.

MOLESKIN: Prevent blisters where friction might create hot spots on your skin.

ANTI-ITCH LOTION: Treat insect stings or topical reactions to plants.

TWEEZERS: Remove splinters and ticks.

NEEDLE OR SAFETY PIN: Drain blisters.

ELASTIC BANDAGE: Prevent swelling of a sprain or immobilize an injured limb.

NONLATEX GLOVES: Prevent exposure to blood or other bodily fluids and prevent the spread of infection.

CPR POCKET FACE SHIELD: Give rescue breaths safely during CPR.

PAPER AND PENCIL: Jot down notes. Track changes over time, to determine if a hiker's condition is improving, declining, or staying consistent. Notes provide more information for a medical worker.

DENTAL FLOSS: Lightweight and doubles as string.

First Aid

Burns

The care and treatment of a burn will depend on how severe it is.

FIRST-DEGREE BURN

Description: Light burn commonly caused by staying out in the sun or touching a hot pot.

Symptoms: Red skin. No blisters or broken skin.

Treatment: Apply soothing ointment or aloe. Take ibuprofen for pain.

SUNBURN   **FINGER BURN**

SECOND-DEGREE BURN

Description: A burn damaging first and second layers of skin.

Symptoms: Deep red skin. Might have blisters. May appear shiny with splotchy white spots.

Treatment: Rinse with clean water and mild soap. Do not break blisters. Apply thin layer of antibiotic ointment or aloe. Dress lightly and loosely with sterile nonstick gauze. Secure gauze with tape well away from burned area. Apply cold compress to relieve some symptoms.

Many second-degree burns can be cleaned and treated in the backcountry. Be sure to check for infection and change the dressing once a day. However, if the burn is on the hands or feet, or anywhere near the face, genitals, or armpits, then immediately evacuate and get checked by a doctor. This is also true when there are burns on more than 10 percent of the body. (For a rough gauge, the skin on the back of you hand is about 1 percent of your body.)

THIRD-DEGREE BURN

Description: Extremely serious burn that goes down to the innermost layer of skin.

Symptoms: White, brown, or black, with deeply charred skin. Area may feel numb because nerve endings have been destroyed.

Treatment: Requires immediate treatment at nearest hospital. Call 911 for help then wrap patient in clean, breathable clothing and prevent dehydration with fluids.

Natural Cold Compresses

If it's winter or you're at high elevation where there are snowfields throughout the summer, then fill a ziplock bag full of snow or ice and use that to help cool the burn.

Blister Treatment

Once you have a blister, treat it as soon as possible to prevent it from becoming bigger and more painful.

If the blister looks flat, then clean it, bandage it, and keep walking. If it's bigger than your adhesive bandages, use gauze and tape so that no adhesive touches the blister. Adhesive will rip the fragile skin when you try to take it off.

Keeping the skin intact is the best bet to prevent infection, but if the blister becomes too painful to keep walking or bubbles up so much that it looks like it will pop on its own, then you'll need to drain it. Sanitize your hands, then wipe the blistered area with an alcohol pad. Sterilize a needle by wiping it down with an alcohol pad or holding it in a flame from a lighter until the needle is glowing red hot. Wipe off any residue with gauze.

When everything is clean, use the needle to puncture the blister in several places around the edges. Don't go too deep or fast with the needle—only poke until you feel a small release. Allow the fluid to drain out, leaving the top layer of skin in place (pressure is not needed or recommended). After the liquid has drained, apply an ointment and cover the area with gauze, making sure you tape it well away from the fragile skin. Keep the area clean and check the blister every day for signs of infection—it's draining yellow or green pus, or the area around the blister is red, swollen, warm, or very painful.

Poisonous Plants

The four most common plants that people have a reaction to on the trail are:

If you have a reaction to a plant, keep the area clean and treat it with corticosteroid cream or calamine lotion, and take an antihistamine as soon as you can.

Sprained Ankle

When you sprain your ankle, remember the acronym RICE.

R stands for *rest*. Depending on the severity of the sprain, that might mean getting carried out to safety.

I stands for *ice*. Collect snow or ice from the trail or stick your leg in a cool creek for relief and to reduce swelling.

C is for *compression*, which limits swelling and restricts potentially more damaging, movement.

E is for *elevation*, which also helps reduce swelling. Rest your leg in a comfortable position about the level of your heart.

There are several ways to wrap a sprained ankle, knee, finger, or wrist to limit motion and reduce swelling. If you are wrapping an ankle, keep the foot at a 90-degree angle. In other words, point your big toe toward your shin when you wrap underneath your foot and around your ankle.

The wrap technique for an ankle includes going under the arch of your foot several times like a stirrup and then bringing the brace together by wrapping a figure eight around the foot and ankle.

If you want to further immobilize the joint, you can also add a splint to your wrap. If you are using a stiff or uncomfortable object as a splint, cushion it with a shirt or bandage before putting it next to your skin to prevent rubbing. Then wrap the splint to limit motion and provide rigidity.

Hypothermia in All Seasons

It doesn't have to be freezing to get hypothermia. It is easy to get hypothermia in cold, wet, and windy conditions. You lose heat twenty-five times faster in water than in air.

Try making a human burrito to warm up a person with hypothermia. Practice this insulation technique with a friend.

WHAT YOU'LL NEED

➤ An insulating layer (groundsheet or sleeping pad), a sleeping bag, other items that would be in your backpack on a hike, and a friend or family member.

STEP 1 Put a groundsheet, sleeping pad, or other insulating item on the ground in a safe place.

STEP 2 Lay a sleeping bag on top and get the "patient" inside the sleeping bag.

STEP 3 Put as many insulating layers as you have on the patient. For example, if you have a hat, put it on them.

Taking notes is an important way to record information when someone is injured in the backcountry. SOAP is an acronym that will help you organize notes about the situation in a way that helps medical responders:

SUBJECTIVE Write about what happened from your point of view. What caused the injury? For example, *twenty-year-old man hurt his arm. Main complaint is pain above the wrist.*

OBJECTIVE Record symptoms and information such as a cut that is bleeding or the patient's heart rate.

ASSESSMENT Make a conclusion based on the info you've recorded.

PLAN State your next steps to address the issues you came across during your assessment. For example, you might stop the bleeding if it is a cut. You could stabilize a fracture. And you could figure out whether the patient needs to leave the backcountry and how that could happen.

Dangerous Wildlife

Snake Bites

The likelihood of getting bitten by a snake on the trail
is extremely low. One way to prevent snake bites is to
examine the surroundings before stopping to take a break or placing
your hands on a rock. If you are bitten there is a good chance the snake is
not venomous. If the snake was venomous, there is also a chance that no
venom was released.

If you were bitten by a venomous snake, limit physical activity as
much as possible to slow the spread of venom. Stay calm and hike slowly to a place
where you can receive help. Remove any jewelry in case of swelling, cover the bite
with a loose bandage, and keep the bite below the heart. If you are able to do so
safely, get a good look at the snake and take a picture so you can describe it to a
medical professional.

Tick bites

Ticks are a concern on many trails throughout the US. While the
majority of tick bites are harmless, there has been an increase in
tick-born illnesses—in particular Lyme disease. These can be difficult
to diagnose. To prevent a tick bite, avoid hiking through tall plants
and grass. You can also tuck your shirt into your pants and your pants
into your socks to keep ticks off your skin. Ticks are deterred by bug
spray. No matter what prevention you take, also perform frequent tick checks by
examining your body and running your hands over any exposed or accessible skin
to detect ticks before they attach.

If you find a tick attached to your skin, clean the area with rubbing alcohol. Then,
grab the tick by its head with a pair of tweezers and pull the whole tick out. Clean
the skin once again with an alcohol pad or soap and water, and monitor the area
over the next few weeks.

TICK CHECK ZONES

HAIR AND HAIRLINE

EARS

BACK OF NECK

ARMPITS

WAIST

BELLY BUTTON

BETWEEN LEGS

BACK OF KNEES

SAFE WILDLIFE DISTANCES

75 FEET (23 METERS)

DEER AND MOST OTHER WILDLIFE

(ABOUT 2 BUS-LENGTHS)

BEARS

300 FEET (91 METERS)

(ABOUT 8 BUS-LENGTHS)

Black Bears

On all fours, black bears are usually 2–3.5 feet tall (0.6–1 meter). They can climb trees, run up to 30 miles (48 kilometers) per hour, and can be different colors. If you come across a black bear *do not* run away, climb a tree, give it food, or play dead.

When it sees you, talk calmly so it knows you are a human. Slowly wave your arms above your head and make yourself look big. If the bear is standing still, slowly move away sideways; if you walk backward, you might trip! But if the bear starts coming toward you, stop and hold your ground.

If a black bear attacks, *do not* play dead. Fight back with a stick, a rock, or whatever you have. Aim your attacks at the bear's face.

Grizzly Bears

A grizzly is larger than a black bear, at 3–5 five feet (1–1.5 meters) tall on all fours, with a distinctive shoulder hump. Like black bears, they can be different colors.

When hiking in grizzly territory, carry bear spray. Also, make noise and hike in a group, to alert bears to your presence and avoid the chance of a surprise encounter. Make extra noise near streams, rivers, and waterfalls. If you come across an animal carcass, leave the area immediately.

If you are attacked by a grizzly bear, use your bear spray. If it continues to charge, play dead (this is the opposite of the advice for a black bear). Keep your backpack on to protect your back. Lie facedown on your stomach with your hands behind your neck. Keep your legs apart to make it more difficult for the bear to flip you over. You want to protect your stomach and vital organs. Try to stay still until the bear leaves. But if the attack continues, there may be a point when you need to fight back. Be very aggressive and direct your attack at the bear's face.

How to Build a Fire

Place some tinder in the middle of your fire ring. From here, you have several options for how to build your fire, depending on the kind of fire you want:

Campfire Flow Chart

Do you have limited firewood or lots?

Little — Lots!

Little: Slower burning fire (which uses less wood)

Lots!: Fire that burns quickly (which uses more wood)

Is it windy? — Are you in a hurry?

Yes — No — Yes — No

LEAN-TO — **LOG CABIN** — **CRISSCROSS** — **TEPEE**

TINDER Small twigs, dry leaves, needles, wood shavings, and bark will catch fire easily but burn quickly!

KINDLING Small sticks (less than one inch thick) placed next to the tinder take longer to light, but will provide the heat needed to ignite larger logs.

FIREWOOD Bigger pieces of wood will keep your fire going until you decide to let it die out. Remember to stack the wood upwind from your campfire.

TEPEE Build a tepee over your tinder with kindling. Make a wide base like a cone, and leave small gaps between each piece and light the tinder. (Airflow is necessary because fire needs oxygen.) After it's lit, add progressively bigger pieces of kindling and then your firewood. Keep the thickest part of each piece at the bottom. This type of fire creates an intense heat and tends to burn quickly.

LOG CABIN Place two logs parallel to each other around the pile of tinder. Then add two more crosswise on top to make a square. Build up the four sides until it resembles a cabin. Place some kindling on top and in the center before you light the tinder. Once this type of fire gets going, it is usually pretty easy to maintain because it disperses the flames around the square and burns slowly.

LEAN-TO The lean-to method is a good choice if it is windy. Place a larger piece of firewood next to your tinder so it blocks the wind. Then put the kindling on top of the tinder, so it is protected from the wind.

CRISSCROSS Get a fire going with just your tinder and gently place the kindling around it in a triangle formation. Then stack your firewood on top in a crisscross pattern.

Shelter

→ Find a nice level spot for your tent, a nearby water source, a good tree to hang a bear bag from, and a good place for campfires.

→ Find flat ground whenever possible, and avoid protruding objects such as rocks, stumps, and roots. Slopes can make sleeping and walking around the campsite difficult. And if it rains, water will run downhill through your campsite. Better yet, look for level ground that is slightly raised, such as a knoll or rounded hill, so you stay high and relatively dry—or at least away from drainage—in heavy rain.

→ Camp a 100 yards (91 meters) away from water sources and away from where you cooked, ate, and ultimately stored your food.

→ Choose a campsite that is not under any hazards such as dead trees or branches that may fall in the middle of the night.

A-FRAME

The simplest tarp configuration is using a rectangular tarp to create an A-frame shelter.

Setting up an A-frame tarp:

STEP 1 Lay out the tarp. Make sure that the four corners of the tarp have cord attached to them. Locate two paracords in the middle of opposite sides of the tarp. If your tarp has no preattached cords or cords only on the corners, run a loose cord under the middle of the fabric.

STEP 2 Tie these cords to nearby trees.

STEP 3 Last, stake out the four corners of the tarp to the ground and voilà! You have an A-frame shelter.

DIAMOND

On a pleasant night with little chance of rain, you might want to set up your tarp in a diamond.

Setting up a diamond tarp:

STEP 1 Lay out the tarp. Make sure that the four corners of the tarp have cord attached to them.

STEP 2 Tie two opposite corners of a square tarp to nearby trees, as high as possible.

STEP 3 Use paracord to stake down the two loose corners as tight as possible.

LEAN-TO

The lean-to design creates three open sides, but still offers substantial protection from wind and precipitation when pitched properly. Arrange the tarp configuration so that the wall of the tarp is facing into the wind or rain as opposed to the awning.

Setting up a lean-to tarp:

STEP 1 Lay out the tarp. Make sure that the four corners of the tarp have cord attached to them.

STEP 2 Find the paracords in the middle of the opposite sides of a square or rectangular tarp. If the tarp has no preattached cords or cords only on the corners, you can run a loose cord under the middle of the fabric.

STEP 3 Use the paracord to suspend the middle of the fabric to chest or waist height and tie each end to a tree.

STEP 4 Step to one side of the suspended tarp and stake the corners on that side to the ground.

STEP 5 Step to the opposite side of the suspended tarp. Place a trekking pole or long sturdy stick under one of the two loose corners and pull the fabric tight. (If your tarp has a grommet or metal hole in the corner, you can place the top of the trekking pole handle on the ground and stick the bottom tip through the grommet.) Then stake the paracord running from that corner to the ground.

STEP 6 Almost there! One more corner to go. Take your second pole and place it underneath the last loose corner of the tarp. Pull the tarp tight and secure the paracord extending from that corner to the ground. Your lean-to tarp is complete with a wall on one side and a roof on the other.

Knots

Here are two common two knots that can be used to tie paracord to the tarp and then secure the paracord to trees or stakes.

BOWLINE

A bowline knot helps you form a loop that will not slip. This creates a spot in the cord that can easily be hooked and unhooked around tent stakes.

STEP 1 Make a loop in the cord so that it looks like a lower case b with the loose end of the cord— the "working end"—resting on top.

STEP 2 Take the working end of the cord behind the neck of the b and then thread it through the backside of the loop.

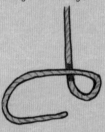

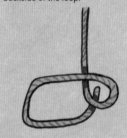

STEP 3 Now bring the cord to the right of the long neck of the b and wrap it around the back of the neck to reach the left side.

STEP 4 Take the working end and thread it through the front of the loop. This time, keep pulling on the cord while also holding the b at the intersection where its long neck meets its big belly. When you are done pulling, you should be left with a sturdy loop and a knot that can easily be untied.

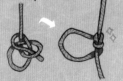

TWO HALF-HITCH

A two half-hitch knot can be used to secure cord to the trunk of a tree. It is secure enough to keep your tarp taut all night, but it can be easily loosened and undone in the morning—even with cold fingers!

STEP 1 Take the cord and wrap it around a tree trunk to make a U shape.

STEP 2 Now take the working end of the cord and place it over the stiff piece of cord to create a loop.

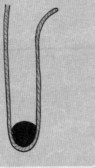

STEP 3 Pull the working end of the cord underneath the stiff piece of cord, and then bring it back above the intersection of cord that you have created so that it is to the right of the intersection and next to the tree trunk.

STEP 4 Repeat step 3 below the existing coil to create the second half hitch, then pull tight.

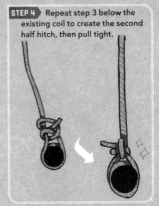

Drinking Water

All water sources are *not* created equal. If you are dehydrated, then use the nearest water source. If you aren't dehydrated, however, be selective about where you collect water. Look for running water sources like mountain springs, rivers, and lakes that are not below roads, farm stock, or developments. Almost all water sources on the trail will need to be treated or filtered before consumption.

OKAY

GOOD

ONLY IF YOU'RE DESPERATE!

YES, PLEASE!

Having too much sediment in your water can break filters and make it taste unpleasant, so you can prefilter water to remove debris before treating it.

WHAT YOU'LL NEED

➤ A water bottle, a bandanna or cloth of some kind, and a natural water source.

STEP 1 Cover the mouth of your water bottle with the bandanna.

STEP 2 Hold the water bottle with the covering under the water until the bottle is full.

STEP 3 Lift the bottle out of the water. Remove the bandanna. The water is not yet safe to drink. But you have removed the grit.

Filtering water removes debris and waterborne illnesses manually. Chemical treatments and boiling will make the water safe to drink, but they don't remove anything. Both are good options in the backcountry.

Boil Your Water

Boiling water for three minutes will kill any living organisms.

Chemically Treat Your Water

There are a variety of different chemicals that can be used to treat water, including iodine and chlorine dioxide. The drawback of chemical treatments is that they take twenty to thirty minutes to purify water, and they can leave an unpleasant aftertaste in your water. Iodine in particular can stain your water bottle a brown color. On the upside, chemical treatments are lightweight, affordable, and easy to use.

Water Filters

There are lots of kinds of filters—pump filters, gravity filters, squeeze filters, and more. But in each, water is forced to travel through a membrane that removes debris and harmful microscopic organisms. The downside is that these filters don't remove viruses, pesticides, or heavy metals. Also, if you use a filter, avoid water with lots of sediment because it can clog or break the filter.

	Boil water	Chemical treatment	UV treatment	Filter
Time needed	Camp stove setup (3 minutes) + bring water to boil (5 minutes) + steady boil (3 minutes) + wait till it cools (7–18 minutes) Total time: 18–29 minutes	Wait 30 minutes	Ready to drink immediately	Ready to drink immediately
Lightweight		✓	✓	✓
Inexpensive (Less than $50)	✓	✓		✓
Removes debris				✓
Taste				Tastes best because it removes debris

Extreme Environments

You might think the best place to cross a river is where it is the most narrow. But that is often where the water is flowing the fastest because it is all being funneled into a tiny area. Often, the widest part of the river will be the safest bet.

If the current is strong, slightly angle your body upstream and step sideways. Take small steps and don't lift your second foot until the first one is secure.

If you are with friends, use a group technique. Groups of three can form a triangle by holding on to one another's waists. Moving together through the water makes you a stronger force against the water. If you have more than three people, form a line or circle by holding on to one another's arms or waists.

How to Read a River

SLOW ● **MEDIUM** ● **FAST**

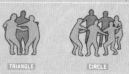

TRIANGLE **CIRCLE**

Frostbite

The first sign of frostbite is cold, red, painful skin, followed by a prickling feeling as the area goes numb. As frostbite progresses the skin will become hard and waxy looking and may turn white or gray.

Like burns, frostbite has three stages—frostnip, superficial frostbite, and deep frostbite. At the superficial stage, your skin may actually start to feel warm before it turns numb again as the damage progresses deeper. With deep frostbite, your joints and muscles may no longer work properly.

If your fingers are feeling numb or tingly, take your gloves off and place your hands under your layers so that they are touching the skin on your belly, armpits, or even your thighs. Whatever you do, don't rub the skin. That can cause more damage if ice crystals have begun to form.

If the skin is hard and waxy, it is already frostbitten. If there's any chance that the skin will refreeze, do not try to thaw it. Refreezing thawed skin will cause even worse damage. Do not use any direct heat like handwarmers on numb skin because they can cause burns if a person can't feel their skin getting too hot. If you have a stove, heat some water to gently thaw the area. Make sure the water is very warm to the touch, but not hot. You can also sip warm liquids to help warm you from the inside. Rewarming should take about thirty minutes. As the skin thaws, you will feel tingling and burning as blood flow returns. Protect the skin from refreezing and do not break any blisters that may have formed.

Sometimes storms sneak up on you in the woods. You might not even realize a storm is imminent until it's suddenly darker, cooler, or windier. If you think a storm might be headed your way, put on your rain gear. If you are stuck in a crouched position in the pouring rain for a while, you will get cold. You can get hypothermia even in temperatures in the 50s if it is wet and windy.

Being close to the ground makes you a smaller target so there is less of a chance of being struck by lightning or a flying object. The lower you are the better, so find a ditch or low-lying area, and lie flat with your hands covering your head. You definitely do *not* want to be any of these places:

→ **In open areas where you are the tallest object**

→ **On a mountain summit**

→ **On a ridge or cliff**

→ **In shallow caves**

→ **Near tall trees or other tall objects**

→ **In gullies, washes, ditches, streams, or any type of water**

→ **Near large boulders or under rock overhangs (lightning can travel along the rocks to reach the ground)**

So what can you do if you get caught in an exposed area with a lightning storm? The first thing to do is to move quickly out of the open, to lower ground if you are high up. Getting below the tree line would be best. Make sure you are not the tallest object in the area. The tallest object often receives a direct strike. Do not seek shelter next to the tallest object, either, because the strike can jump from the tallest object to a person standing nearby. Be aware of dangerous ground currents and do not lie down. Instead, assume the lightning position: Squat down, ideally on your sleeping pad, keeping your weight on the balls of your feet and your feet together. Put your hands over your ears and keep your head low. Stay away from any body of water, which is also a good conductor of electricity.

How Far Away Is That Lightning?

LIGHTING POSITION

When you see lightning flash outside, count how many seconds go by before you hear the thunder. Sound travels one mile in five seconds, so once you have that number, divide it by five. Let's say you see the lightning and get to ten before you hear the thunder: 10 ÷ 5 = 2, so the storm is two miles away. Track the storm with each flash of lightning and rumble of thunder so you can tell whether the storm is moving toward you or away from you. If you are outside and not able to count to ten between a lightning bolt and thunderclap, then assume the lightning position immediately.

ESSENTIAL SURVIVAL SKILLS
IN A **WATERPROOF**
AND **TEARPROOF** BOOK
THAT FITS INSIDE YOUR POCKET!

MADE WITH DURABLE TYVEK MATERIAL!
100% WASHABLE AND **100% FUN!**

QUICK TIPS AND CLEAR
DIAGRAMS FOR:

Navigation

Finding North | Setting Your Bearing

Essentials Kit | First Aid

Dangerous Plants & Animals

Fire | Shelter | Knots | Water

Weather | SOAP Method

US $9.99 / CAN $13.50
ISBN 978-1-250-75467-7

50999 >

9 781250 754677

OddDot.com

OUTDOOR SCHOOL
ANIMAL TRACKS